I0161875

DEDICATIONS

This book is dedicated to the millions of young adults who may have found themselves at a crossroad during or around the first quarter of their life. This book is intended to be my articulation of research and testimony to help you understand where you are, and how to move on. Here's your divine opportunity to re-discover your authentic self.

The Quarter Life Crisis

A Spiritual Journey Back to Self for 20-30 Something Year Olds

Written By:
Kenyon R. Dudley, BS, ORDM, Ptr

Scripture quotations are taken from the *Holy Bible*, New Living Translation, copyright ©1996, 2004, 2007 by Tyndale House Foundation; the *Holy Bible*, King James Version. New York: American Bible Society: 1999 Holy Bible, King James Version, copyright © 1999 by New York: Bible Society; and the *Holy Bible*, Amplified Version, *Copyright © 2015*. Any other citations are listed at the end of this book for reference.

Printed in the United States of America

THIS BOOK IS NOT INTENDED TO BE A HISTORY TEXT. While every effort has been made to check the accuracy of dates, locations, and historical information, no claims are made as to the accuracy of such information.

For book orders, author appearance inquires and interviews, contact author. Contact information is on Contact Page after Table of Contents.

ISBN-13: 978-0998802541 (DP House, Inc.)
ISBN-10: 0998802549

Dudley Publishing
HOUSE

www.dphouse.net

"…this is your opportunity to rediscover yourself."
Kenyon R. Dudley

The Quarter Life Crisis | Kenyon R. Dudley

Table of Contents

KENYON R. DUDLEY does speaking engagements and interviews.
To book please call 678-508-5152, 1-818-660-7083, or email us your inquiry at submissions@dphouse.net.

Join KENYON R. DUDLEY for additional spiritual and practical life lessons via YouTube! New *Vlogs* are uploaded often. Join the spiritual journey to your authentic self.

The Quarter Life Crisis | Kenyon R. Dudley

The Quarter Life Crisis | Kenyon R. Dudley

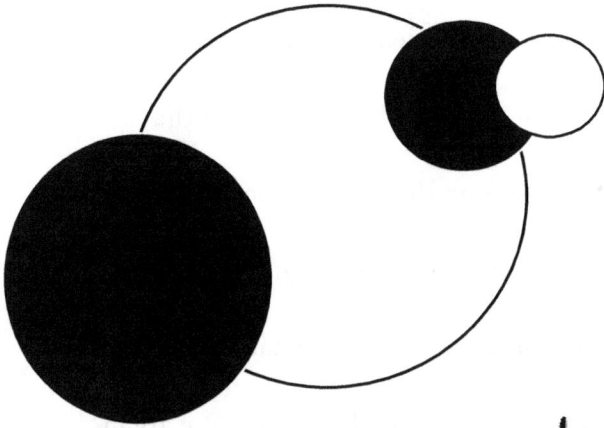

Intro

"Many people die at 25 but aren't buried until they are 75 *(Benjamin Franklin, BrainyQuote.com)*." This notion is riveting. I mean, the thought of the real world being full of zombies is like Michael Jackson's *Thriller* coming to life before our very eyes. But if we'll be honest for a second, you and I both know that this world is full of dead men—*and women*—walking. I'm not referring to necessarily physical death, but perhaps many of us are dead in spirit, dead in cause, or dead in purpose. I'm not saying that we're *lifeless*, meaning that there is no life to look forward to. That would make one just plain suicidal. No, I'm saying that we're simply *separated* from the authentic life for us. We are in one spot, while our real life that we're meant to live is in another spot waiting for us to arrive. It's a matter of ascertaining life; rather than if it exists. I am learning that there is an authentic, peaceful, and happy life for all of us. It *does* exist. We've just got to locate it and seize it.

The world is so full of challenges, turns, twists, and bends that it's easy for *anyone* to get lost in the conundrum of life. Many often fail to reach the maximum of their purpose and goals for this

very reason. I call it *The Great Distractions.*
Distractions are everywhere, and they can often
throw you off course if you're not careful. Thus, is
many of the stories untold by the adults who
struggle with identifying their purpose, knowing
their place in this life, and enjoying every waking
moment. At some point, you just get stuck. I
mean, for no rhyme and no reason at all it seems.
Sometimes, you just get *STUCK!*

As I write this book in my home office, I am
currently twenty-seven years old; and *I am slowly
come out of being stuck. I know. I know.* That's
kind of hard to believe because I'm writing this
book. But the book is a part of my journey to
liberation. And I stress, it's a *journey.* I must
warn you, "I'm not saying that I have this all

together, that I have it made. But I am well on my way, reaching out for Christ, who has so wondrously reached out for me. Friends, don't get me wrong: By no means do I count myself an expert in all of this, but I've got my eye on the goal, where God is beckoning us onward—to Jesus. I'm off and running, and I'm not turning back *(The Message, Philippians 3:14)*. This has become one of my favorite biblical scriptures as I walk as a spiritual body through this natural experience.

What I have learned is that people—especially adults—have mastered the art of dysfunctional functioning. I now realize that—since a child—I had learned how to cope with my inauthentic life by simply going along with the flow. Although there's nothing wrong with going with the flow, it is vital to ensure that the current you're going with is authentically *you*. For many years, I had allowed my relatives, my friends, my church, my religion, my school, and even my culture to influence who I was. Although it is virtually impossible *not* to be influenced by these facets of life, it is vital that you master the art of going beyond these—sometimes—external distractions to listen within. *Within*, is where your spirit dwells. And in spirit is where you can find your truth and authentic self; who God made you to be.

For decades I had either denied myself of listening within or I allowed my spirit to fall subject to the enforced identity of outside sources.

This often-created internal conflict and outside disarray. It was *just this year*—at age twenty-seven—that I had an enlightening moment. I found myself in the Quarter Life Crisis. What is the Quarter Life Crisis? I know. I hadn't heard of it until I was twenty-seven myself. For years, people talked about the Midlife Crisis. They warned, if you take care of your temple, accomplish what you want, and live well then you could potentially avoid the Midlife Crisis. But no one had warned me about the Quarter Life Crisis. This catastrophe "is a period of life ranging from ages between the twenties to thirties, in which a person begins to feel doubtful about their own lives, brought on by the stress of becoming an adult *(Wikipedia)*." But Self.com says it best.

They describe this period of life as a sense of panic that your life—career, relationships, etc.—isn't where you want it to be. I'd say that about sums it up. If you're between the ages of 20-30+ and you're feeling like there *must* be more to your life than this, then *congratulations* you're having a Quarter Life Crisis. If you're suddenly panicking because it seems that everyone else around you are doing well, then *congratulations* you're probably experiencing the Quarter Life Crisis. What about this? Have you started questioning your purpose yet? Are you inundated with the thought that you may be at the wrong job, in the wrong field, or you just may want to become a monk or recluse and not subject yourself to the traditionalism and ritualism of going to church just to go to church? *Congratulations, you know what!*

Don't fret. Your head isn't going to explode or anything like that. Although, it may feel like it at times from all the back and forth uncertainty. However, I have learned to look at this point in life as a blessing rather than an illness or a curse. The intent of this brief book is to show you how I turned my Quarter Life Crisis into a spiritual journey to my authentic self. You don't have to get caught up or stuck. There is a way out of this challenge. To me, that way is finding your way to your authenticity. But you've got to understand that it's just as much a spiritual journey than it is a professional or relational journey. In fact, I believe that one must tap *into* the spirit—*their spirit*—to access their authenticity; and by doing so they will see improvement on all other planes of their life. If you're besieged, that's a clear sign that perhaps God has brought you to this place because you have lost touch of the real you. "All things are lessons that God would have us learn *(Iyanla Vanzant)*." This moment of stress, anxiety, and confusion is a blessing in disguise. Here's your moment to go deep within yourself, the replica of the universe, and find the authentic you. Are you ready for your spiritual journey to the real you?

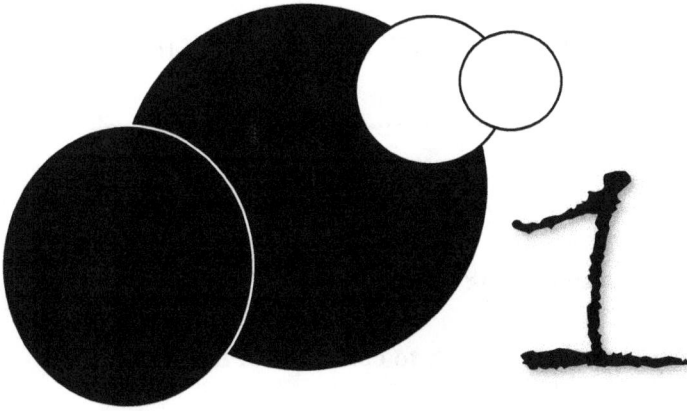

1

Crisis Mode

For over a decade I have struggled with bouts of frustration, depression, and anxiety. There, I said it. I'm a twenty-seven-year-old University student at Mercer, with a nine-to-five-job as a Call Center Supervisor, a husband to the love of my life and father of three *(my second deceased)*. I've done alright for myself; but I can't help but feel that nagging sense of frustration, depression, and anxiety lingering in my subconscious and weighing on my chest at times. Nowadays, it seems to have heightened. The loudness has been a part of the background music of my life since around the age of nineteen. *I am in crisis mode.* And I *have been* for a *very* long time now. But I'm determined to come out; to come out of hiding thus coming out of my pain. Here's my story. A mere bout of what I call the *Adolescence Blues* suddenly turned into young adult struggle. I didn't know it until now, but it's called the Quarter Life Crisis.

Antonio Gramsci utters, "*The crisis* consists precisely in the fact that *the old is dying and the new cannot be born*; in this interregnum a great variety of morbid symptoms appear *(Prison Notebooks, 1971)*." Anyone can become subjected to crisis. *Anyone.* Crisis is no respecter of persons so long as the right formula is present. It is not reserved for the weak or the mentally ill. I find it interesting how Gramsci puts it. Crisis materializes when the old is coming to an end, but the new cannot either be found, articulated, or ascertained. It's in that brief pause of life—the in-between stage of death and reemergence—that frightens us all. It's the lose sense of normal, but the uncertain future that dangles us on a light post where no light shines. The darkness frightens us and drains the living soul out of us.

The Quarter Life Crisis feels like this: you have fulfilled the accomplishment you set out to do in high school. You always wanted to get a degree in Law to become one of the State's District Attorneys. Well, you did that and you've been a

District Attorney for three years now. But suddenly, one day you no longer feel the passion or zeal you once felt for the career. And as you continue to look around and on social media a real hunger for something more arises. Perhaps it's your newfound desire to have children like all your friends. Perhaps it's the revelation that you never wanted to be stuck in a courthouse for the rest of your life anyway. Listen, you're *not* crazy. Your feelings are valid and true. You've simply hit a *pause* in your life. You're at the crossroad of accomplishment and something new. It can be a scary place. Sometimes you feel like you're losing your mind.

Such was my case. As a teenager, I had done things that some adults had not even *began* to do, let alone dream of. I preached my first sermon at the age of ten. I travelled the nation speaking, singing, and briefly acting in shows and on television during my entire adolescent stint. By sixteen, I had performed at the Venetian Hotel in Vegas. At the time I was preparing to become a senior in high school, I had completed all my required courses and was afforded the opportunity to graduate early. On my diploma I'm a graduate of 2007, but I wasn't supposed to walk until 2008. By seventeen I had moved clear across the country to live emancipated in Los Angeles, California. I had made my first ten thousand dollars by eighteen years old, which afforded me to live a heck of a life while I was in SoCal *(Southern California)*. So, there I was at eighteen, seemingly fulfilled. I had done so many wonderful things by this age. Many people, including family either admired me or hated me because of my success. Either way, I was in my glory because I was the *it* person. Then, I immediately hit a transition; or should I say a standstill.

My short-lived success in SoCal came to a screeching halt when my father fell extremely ill to diabetes and high blood pressure. It was obvious my mother needed me back home in Atlanta. And it was even more obvious that they could no longer emotionally or financially support my California dream lifestyle. By nineteen, I had blown my ten thousand dollars and was dependent upon my parents again. So, when my father fell ill, I had no choice. I reluctantly came back home. The only upside to this transition was that I had met a girl who's now my wife. Little did I know that I was about to enter a crisis; the Quarter Life Crisis.

Now that I was back at home in Atlanta, what was I going to do with myself? By now, my identity was wrapped up in movies and television show auditions. I was seldom being called to preach and speak at different places; because I had left to live in SoCal. Many of my connections stopped inviting me places. I initially thought it was because I had lost my charisma and skill. I now understand that it was my lack of relevance. By the time I got back to my hometown, I was now an adult instead of a sensational charismatic teenage speaker and performer. So, those connections no longer saw me as a necessity for their crowds. I was an adult who had a seemingly fulfilled teenage life; and my so-called early blossoming career had crumbled right before my very eyes. Not only that, but the life I once knew— back home—before I left to live in SoCal was crumbling too. My life as I knew was coming to an end; and I was preparing to be ushered into something new. I just didn't know what. And because of fear, lack of funds, lack of collegiate education at the time, among other factors I couldn't see clearly enough to move forward. I became stuck and in crisis. And here's my confession. I've been in limbo until now.

It's funny how life works. At nineteen, I didn't know I was even in a crisis. To be honest, I didn't know what the heck had just happened in my life.

But for the next eight years I was in utter despair. Remember how I said, "adults have mastered the art of functioning in dysfunction?" It wasn't until this year that I realized that I had dated, married, had children, and worked a spectrum of nine-to-five jobs right in the middle of a crisis. I was functioning out of dysfunction. What I learned from this dilemma was that Love carried me through. The love of my wife, the love of my children, and the love of God kept me from losing my *everlasting* mind. See, the Quarter Life Crisis is a spiritual journey. Love is of spiritual substance and origin. It is supernatural in nature. To have the audacity to love—pray and care for—someone who is sick, unable, stuck, at in a *pause* takes spiritual fortitude. One cannot do this in their own strength. Have you ever tried to love somebody who was *just* imperfect? That's exactly what my wife, my children, and God had done for me while going through my calamity. And they're still loving me all the way out of it. Coming out can take time. Remember, it's a journey.

"So, find a heart that will love you at your worst and arms that will hold you at your weakest (*TheDailyQuotes.com*)." This suggestion is vital to your existence and making it through this life challenge. The Quarter Life Crisis doesn't have to be the end of you. You don't have to become one of those adults who spiritually die in your twenties or thirties, but never get buried until your seventies. You don't have to live stuck. You can live past the *pauses* of your life. But you've got to let Love win.

Often—as we dated and courted—my wife and I would argue. I'll say much of it was because of our insecurities and emotional wounds that we both came into the relationship with. But I am a firm believer and a testament that authentic Love—the kind that comes from the Spirit—will heal you and carry you beyond the breakdowns of life. That's exactly what our relationship did. We decided to love one another like Christ loved the Church. Love is the fundamental root cause that has gotten me this far.

Now, I'm not saying you need to go out and marry someone tomorrow. The Love doesn't have to show up in a relationship like that. It could be a brotherly Love that saves you. It could be Love from a friendship that gets you through. The point is, you must find a solid support system of people who will not judge you, but care for you and walk with you through the voyage. What I am suggesting is that you find Love in a friend, a family member, a courtship, a spouse, a child, or most of all in God. This is the pulling force that will bring you along and ultimately to the end of your crisis mode.

Peace in the Pause

I have learned to find contentment and peace in *every* pause of life. And I stress the word *find* because contentment and peace   is not always visible, yet it *is* always readily available. Having peace means a journey –an expedition—of discovery. It's up to you to access it.

You can access peace through solitude, prayer, and the feeding of your soul and spirit. *That's it!*

You access peace through the solitary and reverent moments in your life. Guess what that means? That's right. There's no way around it. You're going to have to slow down—come to a screeching stop even—and take the time to *just* be. Just be with the universe; with God. I must admit, this can be hard to do living in our age of dispensation. For generations we have made strides—especially in America—to become more technologically savvy, more innovative, and quicker in everything we do. For the past ten years we've only gotten faster and busier due to the access that the Internet has given us at our fingertips. Technological phenomenon such as social media, smartphones, and other technologies have aided in our innovation. Yet, as a result, it has also had an adverse effect on our societies. Many people—especially millennials—do not have the time or mind to slow down and conduct inner reflection. We are constantly going; and we never take the time to steep our souls, breath, and simply have a *come to Jesus* with ourselves. This puts us at a disadvantage. Most of us aren't ready when life turns, because we are too busy living fast and inauthentically. We are the smartest and quickest generation, but there is no substance to us. We have been deemed as the least spiritual generation yet. Wonder why things such as the Quarter Life Crisis is such on a rise?

It is extremely vital that we see the importance of removing as many external forces and distractions as possible. I have learned that we *must* develop ritual that will steep our souls; and it *must* involve solitude. Do this until your entire life becomes a living breathing atmosphere of worship and peace. "Sometimes I'm alone, but never lonely. That's what I've come to realize. I've learned to love the quiet moments. The Sunday mornings of life; where I can reach deep down inside, or out into the Universe. I can laugh until I cry, or I can cry away the hurt *(Private Party, India Arie)."* Sacred words from one of my anthems. When's the last time you had a good cry, huh? Tell me, when's the last time you danced in the spirit? I know this sounds bizarre for the contemporary, but when's the last time you sang to yourself? I mean, *really* sang a love song to yourself and to the Spirit of God inside you? See, it's in these moments where you can connect with God on a much deeper level than just going to church, going to synagogue, or showing up at the mosque. It's in your own secret quiet moments of worship and gratitude where the Spirit of God can manifest more vividly and speak to you about your life. Much like India, I have always loved the quiet moments of life. It's a place and a space where I can declutter my thoughts, settle my soul, awaken my spirit, and rest in the All-Knowing. I can say that I've committed myself to so many still moments that my entire life is now becoming a Sunday morning.

Remember, your release and graduation from the Quarter Life Crisis isn't going to come just because you desire it. You're going to have to put some work in on this spiritual journey. Peace and joy doesn't just come in the morning because you ask for it. They come in the morning because light has broken through the clouds and shewn forth. In a spiritual sense, light is revelation, clarity, knowledge, wisdom, and understanding. Peace can only fill your soul and life when you have taken the time to seek the wisdom of the morning. Things such as knowledge and understanding are all spiritual nuggets that can be naturally applied to your life; but you can only access them as you live more aware of the Spirit. For, awareness of the Spirit is perfect solitude.

FOMO

I have discovered that the main culprit that triggered my first quarter crisis was the infamous *FOMO*; fear of missing out *(UrbanDictionary.com)*. A phenomenon that most millennials are experiencing right now, if they were honest. Both downward and upward social comparison is prevalent and at an all-time high. The comparison—that is often promoted by social media nowadays—is the reason I spiraled

out of control. I couldn't help but compare my life to the lives of friends and loved ones. And I was doing this *every* day. Often, I'd plunge into a subtle depression or even rage and anger, because the friends I saw on social media seemed as if they were doing better than me. And I couldn't fathom it. I couldn't grasp the concept of how I was number one out of the class, but suddenly became the last and the least among them all. It's terrifying and downright embarrassing. For most of this journey I have had to work through so many emotions, it's not *even* funny. I can remember my wife looking at me one day with a bewildered face—*we were on the couch*—as I spiraled into one of my crying and depressing rants. Our third child had just been born about a week prior. At a moment where I was supposed to be at the height of happiness, I couldn't help but be overcome with grief and sorrow. I was too busy comparing my life to that of the other guys who had graduated high school with me. And yes, I was a grown man throwing a temper tantrum on *my* couch in front of *my* wife. Thankfully, she loves me and judges me not. *Ha!* Now there's your example of having a strong support system and love surrounding you during this time of highs and lows. I was at one of my worst moments in the Quarter Life Journey, yet she sat and listened without judgement. In fact, she even prayed for me.

Beware! One of the main culprits that can trigger your anxiety and frustration while on this journey of figuring things out and finding yourself is *comparison*. You must expel every situation that may cause you to compare yourself. Although, comparing is inevitable to your growth—until you can get your emotions under control and your confidence in tact—*do not* put yourself in that type of predicament. And *do not* allow anyone else to place you in that type of position either; *not even family.*

I have a few practical ways that I've learned to expel the awkwardness of comparison and build my confidence. I call them my 7 Mountain Movers:

- ✓ ONE: Each morning, write down at least 40 *I Am* statements. Then recite them aloud.

✓ TWO: Keep a daily or weekly *Gratitude Journal* by writing all the things you're grateful for in that day or week. Then read them aloud.

✓ THREE: Write down at least 30 blessings, positive declarations, or decrees concerning your life. Then recite the same 30 aloud each night before you go to bed.

✓ FOUR: When someone begins to compare you to someone else, stop them right at mid-sentence and change it. Respectfully yet boldly, say who you are and let the person know that you are uniquely designed.

- ✓ **FIVE: Surround yourself with people who honor who you *really* are, and not who they *want* you to be.**
- ✓ **SIX: Discontinue anything that makes you feel inadequate to the point of depression, anger, unhappiness, sadness, or any other negative emotion.**
- ✓ **SEVEN: Pray consistently to God; thanking God for your ability to possess clear vision of who you are and the courage to live that out.**

Mountain Mover #ONE

DISCLAIMER: Please excuse me. I don't mean to get too mythical and spiritual here; but I *did* state—earlier in this work—that this is a spiritual journey to freedom. To walk through this

devastating time in your life—*at some point*—you're going to have to sit back and realize that this is more spiritual than it is natural. And there is just as much spiritual disarray going on in your life as it is psychological, professional, and such.

The first mountain mover—*the 40 I Am Statements*—will give you authority over negative thoughts, perceptions, and images impressed upon your psyche and your spirit. Did you know that Media has become one of the greatest mediums by which negative perceptions are formed and broadcasted? *Go figure!* Before Media—written and printed works, radio, and television—there was the spoken word. Many ideas, thoughts, rituals, and other traditions were passed down from generation to generation by the tongue. Which is why I consider the tongue one of the most powerful and ancient weapons in combat and warfare. Listen, if you're going to win this battle in your mind and heart, the *first* thing you're going to have to do is broadcast something different. Send more positive signals to your brain, rather than these negatives signals given off by distracting billboards, movies, television programming, manipulative leaders, and such. Now, I'm not saying you need to throw out all of the T.V.'s in the house. But *I am* saying, be your own censor and your *own* producer of your *own* positive programming. You must begin to speak otherwise. Use your tongue to re-write the script of your cognitive beliefs. These 40 statements will get you in the habit of hearing more positive things about yourself and your life. And eventually your heart will catch up with the words. You will begin to believe what you're hearing—*beyond the negativity*—and your perception and reality will begin to change.

Mountain Mover #TWO

The second mountain mover—*the Gratitude Journal*—will help you conquer your need to devalue celebration. I was raised in a society where celebration was foreign. I'm not referring to birthday parties and anniversaries. The celebration of one's hard work and presence, is what I mean. Where I come from, many of the fathers didn't receive *Thank You* cards for Father's Day. *Heck!* They barely received a *Thank You* from their children *any* time of the year. Men were devalued and thought of as nothing worth celebrating. It was a place where—if you did something *extraordinary*—it wasn't celebrated as much as the fella who had just gotten released from prison. Somehow, his making it out of the pen and back onto the streets was more valuable and worth celebrating than a kid who had made it into the Robotics Club. And many things simply weren't celebrated *at all* because the moment celebration happened, a disappointment would manifest. We were often afraid to celebrate from the fear of what was to come next.

But keeping a *Gratitude Journal* will get you in the habit of celebrating. Celebration should be the norm in your life, no matter what comes next. *Celebrate everything. Everything.* Big or small. Get in the habit of being grateful. Don't you know that gratitude and celebration puts you in a space that allows you to attract more goodness? The more you find things to be grateful for in your life, the more the Universe *(God)* will offer up more things in your life to be grateful for. *It's just a principle.* It's a part of the Law of Attraction. As you master this principle, you will begin to see great moments and opportunities show up in your life more often. But they won't show up until you are genuinely grateful for *your* life. *Not someone else's.*

Mountain Mover #THREE

The *30 Blessings*—that you write down and recite every night before bed—is a way to keep a visible track of your spiritual repertoire. I like to call it *the process of taking a view of the stock of your soul* to see if it's well balanced and diversified. By listing and reciting these *30 Blessings* or declarations you're able to see what's top priority to your true self. "A good man out of the good treasure of his heart brings forth good; and an evil man out of the evil treasure of his heart brings forth evil. For out of the abundance of the heart his mouth speaks (New King James Version Bible, Luke 6:45)." Is it money, identity, a career, your faith, a job, family, or is it all the above? What is it that's most important to your true self? Listing the next *30 Blessings* that you're trusting God to manifest in your life will give you an opportunity to see what you *really* desire. *Beware!* As you write, you may conclude that some things are *just* not that important to you anymore. *It's natural!* Life changes, and your priorities change. Perhaps the things you thought you wanted just don't fit in the grand scheme and scope of your life anymore. Decide of if the things listed are truly in alignment with your inner self and purpose. If they *are* and you're still witnessing frustration, then you may have some external adjustments to make. If the things listed *aren't* in alignment with who you really are, and they are simply ideas forced upon you; then cross those things off the list and replace them with something more authentically you. Remember, you always want the stock of your soul to be balanced, diversified, but most importantly always reflecting who you really are inside Indeed, the balance *comes* from how authentic each thing is on your list.

Mountain Mover #FOUR

Stopping someone from comparing you to someone else is one of the greatest gifts you'll ever give to yourself while on this Quarter Life Crisis journey. These are the moments where you *really* get to educate everyone and everything around you—while reminding yourself—of who you truly are.

Your fourth mountain of obstruction is education, and I don't mean conventional knowledge or scholastic methods and themes. I mean, the education of who you *really* are. Most people will never know who you are until you educate them. One of my biggest mistakes was assuming that—since I was born into my family— they automatically knew exactly who I was and how I operated. *WRONG!* You must *tell* people who you are. That's why it's vital that *you* know who you are first. Another sad mistake I made was that I thought I automatically knew who I was inside. Surely you shouldn't have to do any homework to seek out who you really are inside. After all, you're with yourself 24/7. I believed this myth until crisis and trauma started hitting me back to back. Listen, crisis will help you understand if you're really in touch with your spirit and soul. I never knew how well I could cuss until I got in a crisis. I never knew that I would jump out of a moving vehicle until I got under enough pressure and stress to do so. The point is, *you've got to educate yourself* and those around you. Do some soul searching, and when you find that true and authentic person please tell yourself and those around you. If you get angry easily when someone uninvitedly shows up at your house, then tell them that in a nice and respectable way. If you can't handle late night movies on cable while you're at home by yourself, then announce that as you tell yourself to go to bed before 10 PM.

This has got to be one of the most important practices I give you. This is going to require you to be honest. The divine opportunity here—that you haven't been aware of until now—is that you haven't been totally honest with yourself. That's a big part of the reason you ended up right here in this crisis. I had to get clear of this myself as well.

Because I did not know who I was—and because I failed to educate myself and others around me—I ended up saying *yes* to a lot of things that I really meant *no* to. I ended up accepting a lot of things that I really didn't want to accept. This did nothing but throw me into a conclusion of stress, angst, and pain. I would often feel left abandoned and abused. I was an open target for spiritual and emotional trauma and abuse. But it was because I wasn't educated on who I was and what I stood for. In essence—know thy values—know thyself.

Mountain Mover #FIVE

Mountain mover #5 is: Surrounding yourself with people who honor who you *really* are. What I really should have said was, "Surround yourself with people who *compliment* who you are."

"Then His mother and brothers came to Him, and could not approach Him because of the crowd. And it was told Him *by some,* who said, 'Your mother and Your brothers are standing outside, desiring to see You.' But He answered and said to them, 'My mother and My brothers are these who hear the word of God and do it *(New King James Version Bible, Luke 8:19-21).*'" The Great Prophet—*and who I consider the Son of God, God incarnate—Jesus* was at a gathering one day preparing to teach. The account can be found in the New Testament of the Hebrew scriptures. There was such a great crowd around him that when Jesus' biological mother and siblings came to see him they couldn't get beyond the outside of the place where Jesus was. Wanting to see him, they sent word that they had arrived, but Jesus failed to come out to see them. His reason was just as much a slap in the face as his failure to go out to greet them. He questions the people inside. "Who are my real family members?" Then he tells them. "My true family are those who love God and do what I do; obey Him." *My goodness*, what a great example of the point I'm making now!

A great deal of your frustration—in this Quarter Life Crisis—*could be* that you have connected and surrounded yourself with individuals who do not honor who you really are. They do not compliment your identity. And they do not exemplify your true and authentic self. Let me ask you a question. If you're an artist, then why are you wasting your valuable time taking up

Biology as a major? If you're a scientist, then why are you trying to make a living drawing pictures on a t-shirt? Don't waste your time or energy on doing *anything* that doesn't align with your destiny and authentic purpose. And don't align yourself with anyone who doesn't compliment the same. It's a waste of your energy, your time, and your grace. My wife taught me this lesson.

So, if you have aligned yourself with a people who are not your true spiritual family members then it's time you evaluate parting ways. I'm not saying that they must look like you or be just like you. That would mean surrounding yourself with clones. That's not the idea I'm making. What I am saying is that it's important you lock arms with the person or people who are going in the same direction as you are. What is their sole—*or soul*—

purpose and mission in life? This is the question

you must ask before you join forces with them or

the initiative on any level. You'll save yourself a lot

of heartache, headache, and misery. If the

girlfriend or boyfriend isn't going in the same

direction divorce the relationship and move on;

and cut out all of that arguing. You're doing

nothing but building more stress and tension in

your life, thus pushing yourself further and further

into crisis.

Lastly, please understand that just because you

must let them go doesn't mean that they're bad

people. So, don't broadcast them in such a

dishonorable way. Jesus' biological mother and

siblings had done nothing wrong. They were

simply being themselves. But their calling wasn't the same as Jesus'. Jesus had another calling and another mission. *That's it!* You've *got* to understand that no one is bad *for* you. They may just simply be bad *with* you. There's no *cause* bad *for* you, it may just bad *with* you. Find your place, find your people and thrive. It's time to evaluate your spiritual family. Who's in your circles? Perhaps you need to start rearranging or cutting ties. I won't lie. This *will* hurt. And it might sting a little. But the aftermath and afterlife is worth the temporary surgical removal. Peace and freedom is beyond the separation.

Mountain Mover #SIX

The sixth mountain mover deals with the mountain of government. When I refer to government, I am referring to the systematic structure of your life. Have you ever asked yourself, "What governs me?" Is it people's opinions? Is it money? Is it career status? Or is it your inner self, your true purpose, your tenacity to serve the world and God as your highest self? In other words, what is your motivation for being? I can tell you that my motivation for being is simply pleasing God and serving the world in the best positive way I can. I understand that I'll do this by being my true and authentic self always. That's the motive and intention that governs me. All else is secondary to me. *It truly is.* So, I have learned to start making decisions and to start building relationships from this clear intent.

As I matriculated through my twenties, I have realized that I'm not worried about making lots of money. I am convinced that I am already wealthy both in spirit and in the natural. All I should do is access it. I've learned that status doesn't really matter, so long as I'm effective. But what *really* matters is if I got a chance to let my true light shine, if I could be a positive example, or change someone's life for the better with the words I spoke or wrote? And the ultimate, did I please God with my life? So, I had to take a real inventory of who and what I had connected with. Then I had to myself ask, "Why?" Why am I connected to this thing or this person? Why am I connected to this cause? Does it align with my purpose? Does it align with my authentic intention? If not, I've got to let it or them go. When you check your motives, and begin to re-structure your life based upon what's not authentic and what is, you do yourself a real service there. Many have hit rock-bottom in the Quarter Life Crisis such as I have. They are angry, frustrated, and ready to give up; but they *just don't realize* that most of the frustration is coming from either unclear or inauthentic intentions. Unclear or inauthentic intentions will manifest everything in your life that's the direct opposite of who you really are. That's what causes a person to feel depressed, sad, and even inadequate. This may be you too. Get rid of all the people and things that make you feel this way. That's a sure sign that you've been unclear with your motives and your intentions.

Mountain Mover #SEVEN

The seventh mountain mover pertains to the mountain of spirituality. *Let's face it!* We all could use a little more time to tap into the Spirit. When it all boils down to it, you're probably flailing out of control because your spiritual life isn't as strong as it *could* be. I had been preaching and conducting motivational speeches for at least a decade when I turned twenty. By then I was fully immersed in the Quarter Life Crisis, but I didn't know it yet. And little did I know that my faith and spirituality was going to be challenged *BIG TIME!* Until then, I thought I had a pretty decent prayer life. I thought I was quite solid in my faith and beliefs. My core values seemed to be clear and strong, but something else was wrong. I realize now, I had been living a lie. The church I had

attended and served for at least fifteen years prior

had lost my interest years before I reached twenty

years old. But I stayed out of loyalism and

tradition. Truthfully, I was miserable and

unfulfilled. My prayers and solitude had become

mundane rituals—that at times—was only for

bragging rights. And I thought I was clear on what

I believed in, but if somebody asked me I couldn't

even dissect the Bible by divisions. I had the form

of Godliness, but I was denying the power of true

spirituality *(King James Version Bible, 2*

Timothy 3:5).

How's your spiritual life? Ask yourself this

question in solitude, and wait for your spirit to

answer. After about five to ten minutes of stillness

you should begin to experience your brain pushing up every answer from your subconscious. You *know* that you haven't fasted and believed like you desire to. You *know* that you must take more time to feed your spirit. You *know* that you haven't served anything higher than yourself since college. I'm not talking about adopting a religion or dogma. Religion is good for social construct, but one must be in touch with their spiritual side of life first before they can adopt a religion. If not, they run the risk of becoming rigid, dogmatic, and traditionalistic without a purpose. Without a solid since of your *own* spirituality, you will become of non-effect and lost in religion.

I think it's *high time* you saw this crisis as a spiritual opportunity with practical symptoms. It's a chance to deal with the underlying issues of your soul from the seat of the Spirit. This means, you've *got* to start empowering and feeding your soul and spirit. You've *got* to start tapping into the Divine through prayer, meditation, and solitude. I do this each day I wake. It has become so secondary to me that I'm doing some of these things while I go about my day. Each day—all day—I'm praying within myself, talking to God, taking deep breaths, communing with the Spirit, listening and hearing what my inner spirit is saying. I'm even taking lunches and breaks to read and listen to things that will motivate, inspire, uplift, and even feed my soul and spirit. Al sorts of things. Although I do believe in Jesus Christ as Savior, I even study various religious and spiritual traditions to understand their perspective and interpretation of God and life. I would be a fool to believe that God is interpreted in *only* one way. We have too many cultures for that.

So, I beseech you to elevate your mind and tap into the Spirit. You'll understand that God is much higher and much bigger than religion and even interpretation. God is the Universe, the cosmos, the trees, God is in every human being. God is everything. To attempt to limit or label God is like putting Him in a glass box. You can see that God doesn't fit, yet you place the limits on the Divine anyway.

As you tap deeper into the Spirit, you begin to understand that God is bigger than your current state of affairs and awareness. And God is grander than your mere aspirations to be like someone else.

You have your own place in the Kingdom, and you

do not have to settle for being a carbon copy. Tap

into the All-Knowing, and feed off God's infinite

wisdom. It's in this place where you will find

yourself and peace for your weary souls.

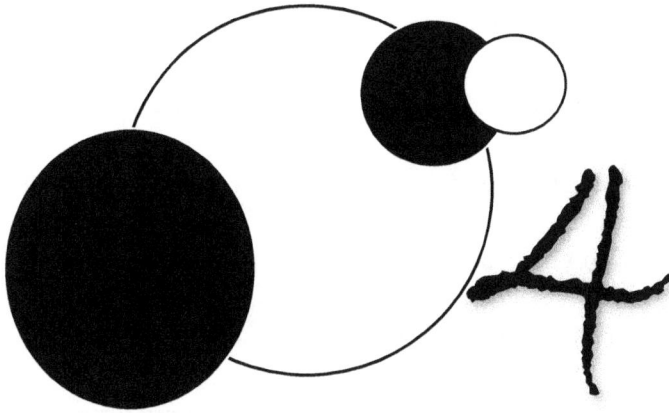

Divine Opportunity

To Leverage or Succumb? That is the question as you stand at your crossroad right now. Let's be honest—if you're at this point of the book—you probably still have questions about where the heck you're going in life? So far, we've covered what you may be experiencing and why. But let's take some time to explore the *where.* Where do you go from here with your life? Do you allow the never-ending questions in your head, the pressures of your parents, or the uncertain feelings of the future take over you until you've balled up in a knot? Do you stay stuck in this transition forever? Or do you tap into who you really are—through spiritual and practical discovery—and then *JUMP*? My friend, I'd say it's high time for you to *JUMP!*

Jumping is another way of saying leverage the crisis. Instead of acting as if it's a crisis, you should change your perspective. Look at this moment in your life differently. Look at it as a divine opportunity. Spirit has brought you to this moment for a reason. And if you choose, Spirit will bring you through this moment; and you'll come out stronger, more authentic, and better than ever. If you would see it this way, you'll realize that you have been offered a divine opportunity to choose better.

"Meet Robert MacNaughton, the cofounder and CEO of the Integral Center in Boulder, CO, an organization that is at cutting edge of personal and relational development. Through MacNaughton's work he has helped tens of thousands create a massive impact in their lives and relationships. However, this would never have been possible for MacNaughton if he hadn't *rerouted* his life at the crucible of a quarter-life crisis. Like all millennials in a quarter-life crisis, *he had a choice to make: to succumb deeper to the depression, or to leverage the pressure as a force for change (Forbes Under 30, Jules Schroeder)*." As I read this piece of Schroeder's article on the Quarter

Life Crisis, I couldn't help but think to myself, "Now here's a guy who blatantly decided to be bold and just *JUMP!*" He took—what could've been—a depressing and debilitating moment in his life and squeezed some positive out of it. Simply put, he tapped into who he really was, let go of all the external forces of impression that would deem him as inauthentic, and he changed the trajectory of his career thus changing his life in the long-run. It sounds simple, but I'm sure this had to be a daring time for him. As I read along, I understood that MacNaughton was surrounded by people who simply went along with the flow—inauthentically—which could most definitely make change hard.

This could be you too. Perhaps, you're surrounded by a world of people who have succumb to their fate, rather than leveraged their crossroad moments as a divine opportunity for better. Or perhaps you're like me. You too have seen people simply make the JUMP, but there's still a fear within that's holding you hostage. No matter where you stand on this issue, the spiritual lesson is still the same. The moment that you're experiencing right now isn't really a crisis, it's a divine opportunity to choose truth. *Your truth!* Complaining, crying, envying others' success, pouting, pretending to be someone else, and all the other unhealthy habits will get you nowhere. At this intersection called the Quarter Life Crisis, you're going to have to choose your truth and authenticity over anything and anyone else. You're going to have to take that spiritual walk back to the real you and embrace *that* person. The practical changes that you begin to make, the people you begin to connect with or disassociate with, the job that you plan to leave, the business that you're planning on starting, the degree that you choose to complete, all the actions that you decide to take from here on *must* be in alignment with your truest and highest self. God can only bless the authentic you, *not* the you that you pretend to be or envy to be. *You're here!* You're at your first quarter crossroad of life. Life doesn't have to end here. Depending on how you look at it, *life is just getting started!* Don't miss the

moment of your miracle simply because you fail to live in your truth.

05

Live in the Now!

Carpe diem! One of my favorite quotes. Written 23 BC by the Roman Poet _Horace_ in his work _Odes (Wikipedia)._ The Latin aphorism has been my proverb for some time now as I've come to the end of my divine opportunity to choose a better life _(the process formerly known as my Quarter Life Crisis)._ After losing countless days to worry, anxiety, and stress I've learned that it's just not worth it. I have witnessed too many close friends and relatives lose their life and go to the grave full. When I was a Junior in high school, I was one out of three students chosen to join a summer scholar program called the *Beacons and Rays of Light Institute*. I'm not sure if they're still around, but it was one of the best moments of my life. The facilitators were very strategic in their tactics that summer before our Senior year. They primed, shaped, and molded our hearts and mind to be leaders and pillars in our communities and the world. Within those few short months they taught us the art of public speaking, how to choose a college by taking us on collegiate tours, among other things. I can vividly remember one assignment we were given. We had to write an essay and recite it on one of the college campuses that we toured. The prompt? *"Who Do You Want to Be Remembered As?"* I can still hear me reciting mine now. I can still see me standing in the middle of one of Florida A&M's basketball gyms as I recited my thoughts to the scholar participants and collegiate students that stopped and stared. The essay was spoken so well that the Directors asked me to recite it again in front of the parents and community leaders that would attend our end-of-the-summer banquet. I can still remember the best piece in the entire essay.

"When it's all said and done—when I die—I want to go in the grave empty. I want to live so well that I give all of myself to serve my purpose, the people that I meet, and my God. I want people to say, "He's finished his task.

He's completed his course. There is no more to him, because he used every ounce of his God-given gift and calling to serve well. And that calling is to serve God by saying something that will change someone else's life for the better."

I still come to the verge of tears when I speak those words aloud. Every fiber in me believes that this is exactly what I'm supposed to be doing. I will admit—somehow—I lost sight of that. But because of God's strategic and infinite wisdom and grace, I was brought to a divine opportunity to re-choose and re-embrace the real me.

If you've gotten nothing else from this body of work, it is my prayer and intention that you leave with this. Live NOW! Live out your truest self and purpose. Don't lose time by worrying about tomorrow. For tomorrow has enough cares of its own *(King James Version Bible, Matthew 6:34)*. Don't lose sleep trying to do it someone else's way. You will only be remembered by doing it *your* way. Plus, doing it your way gives you the fulfillment and joy.

So, stop right now and breath in deeply. Now let it out. From this moment forward, choose to do it *your* way. The way that God has given it to *you*. To me, that's the essence of Carpe diem *(seizing the day)*. Take your life for what its divinely meant to be, and walk in that level of truth. As you practice this way of life, I guarantee that you'll begin to live in peace.

"My all-time favorite animated movie as a child was The Lion King. In fact, I still love this body of work as an adult. I love the film, the musical adaptation, I love all-things Lion King. The most memorable line was spoken by the great spiritualist and village prophet, Rafiki. He says to young adult Simba, "The question is, 'Who are you?'" The moment you find out the answer to this question is the moment you start to live."

-Kenyon R. Dudley

References

(references in order that you read them; not alphabetical)

Intro:

"Benjamin Franklin Quotes." *BrainyQuote*, Xplore,

www.brainyquote.com/quotes/quotes/b/benjaminfr1299

49.html.

"Bible Gateway." *Philippians 3:14-16 MSG - - Bible*

Gateway,

www.biblegateway.com/passage/?search=Philippians%

2B3%3A14-16&version=MSG.

"Quarter-Life crisis." *Wikipedia*, Wikimedia Foundation, 26

Sept. 2017, en.wikipedia.org/wiki/Quarter-life crisis.

Capretto, Lisa. "Iyanla And Oprah Reflect on Their Rift

and Lessons Learned in Challenging Times (VIDEO)."

The Huffington Post, TheHuffingtonPost.com, 24 July

2013, www.huffingtonpost.com/2013/07/24/iyanla-

oprah-rift-lessons n 3641834.html.

"All things are lessons that God would have us learn. -

Iyanla Vanzant." *All things are lessons that God would*

have us learn. Iyanla Vanzant,

www.quotemaster.org/qd91911e5f67f5b1db279d8d7fb1
0cd1c.

Chapter 1:

Gramsci, Antonio, and Joseph A. Buttigieg. *Prison
notebooks.* Columbia Univ. Press, 1971, 2011.

"Arms That Will Hold You." *The Daily Quotes,* 21 Sept.
2015, thedailyquotes.com/find-arms-that-will-hold-
you/.

Chapter 2:

Private Party. Songwriters: INDIA ARIE, BRANDEN
BURCH, RICHARD JOHNSON JR., JOHN
HOWARD III

© Peer music Publishing, Warner/Chappell Music, Inc.

For non-commercial use only.

Data From: Lyric Find

Chapter 3:

"Fomo." *Urban Dictionary,*

www.urbandictionary.com/define.php?term=fomo.

"The Seven Mountains." *Ray Edwards*, 4 Sept. 2013,

rayedwards.com/the-seven-mountains/.

OWN. "Iyanla: The Powerful Advice That Boosts Your Self

Esteem | #OWNSHOW | Oprah Online." *YouTube*,

YouTube, 14 Sept. 2015,

www.youtube.com/watch?v=0j6kxvDuFMk.

Pardon Our Interruption, www.oprah.com/oprahs-

lifeclass/oprah-on-the-importance-of-her-gratitude-

journal-video.

"Bible Gateway." *1 Thessalonians 5:17 KJV - - Bible

Gateway*,

www.biblegateway.com/passage/?search=1%2BThessal

onians%2B5%3A17&version=KJV.

"Bible Gateway." *2 Timothy 3:5-7 KJV - - Bible Gateway*,

www.biblegateway.com/passage/?search=2%2BTimoth

y%2B3%3A5-7&version=KJV.

Chapter 4:

Schroeder, Jules. "Millennials, This Is What Your Quarter-

Life Crisis Is Telling You." *Forbes*, Forbes Magazine, 8

Sept. 2016,

www.forbes.com/sites/julesschroeder/2016/09/08/millenn

ials-this-is-what-your-quarter-life-crisis-is-telling-

you/#428cdff3262d.

Chapter 5:

"Carpe diem." *Wikipedia*, Wikimedia Foundation, 5 Oct.

2017, en.wikipedia.org/wiki/Carpe_diem.

"Bible Gateway." *Matthew 6:34 NIV; KJV - - Bible*

Gateway,

www.biblegateway.com/passage/?search=Matthew%2B

6%3A34&version=NIV%3BKJV.

cornbugles. "The Lion King - Simba & Rafiki (English)."

YouTube, YouTube, 3 Mar. 2008,

www.youtube.com/watch?v=71_p8P_PVXo.

About the Author

Scientifically trained in Psychology, but passionately driven
as a creative, a speaker, and a spiritual teacher. Kenyon R.
Dudley is the Co-Owner and Editor-in-Chief of DP House,
Inc. He has experience that spans across the borders of
ministry, media and publishing, arts and entertainment,
and business.

Kenyon R. Dudley began preaching on platforms at the age
of ten (10). He has since then been officially ordained a
Minister of the Christian Gospel in 2006 and has served as
an Associate Pastor between 2010-2014 at Heart to Heart
Ministries. Growing tired of *church as usual.* Kenyon left the
church he currently served in 2017 to set out on his own
spiritual path and journey that some might say is
unconventional. His motive was to access his authentic self
and the authentic presence of God beyond traditionalism.

Dudley's spiritual influence and greatness encompasses the
art of publishing. Kenyon R. Dudley started his collegiate
career pursuing a major in Broadcast Journalism and has
always exuded a passion for such. He currently serves as

the Editor-in-Chief of Dudley Publishing House *(known as DP House, Inc.)* where he currently manages the publishing process for authors' manuscript accounts.

Kenyon R. Dudley has also garnered experience in the world of arts and entertainment; having served as the personal assistant the talent manager of Carter Entertainment *(Los Angeles, California)* and Sheer Talent Management Group *(Los Angeles, California, and Atlanta, Georgia)*. He has had his share of being behind the scenes, in front of the camera, and on-stage as he starred in the feature film *Bigfoot*, a nationally syndicated *Click It or Ticket* commercial, and more. He has also had the opportunity to write and Executive Produce his own gospel album in 2007.

Kenyon R. Dudley's sole mission is to speak to the heart and mind of people; assisting them with actualizing their authentic self, their dreams, and embracing a very real, relevant, and relatable God. He plans to accomplish this mission with his family: wife *(Jasmine B. Dudley)*, daughter *(Reagan K. Dudley)*, and son *(Julian K. Dudley)*.

@Kenyon Dudley | www.kenyonrdudley.com | (678)-508-5152

www.dphouse.net

www.ingramcontent.com/pod-product-compliance
Lightning Source LLC
Chambersburg PA
CBHW060132050426
42448CB00010B/2091